Old Black Rocking Chair

Old Black Rocking Chair

Recollections and Poems

Author
Violetta Peters

Acclaim Press
MORLEY. MISSOURI

Acclaim Press
— Your Next Great Book —

P.O. Box 238
Morley, MO 63767
(573) 472-9800
www.acclaimpress.com

Book Design: Devon Burroughs
Cover Design: M. Frene Melton

ISBN-13: 978-1-942613-41-1
ISBN-10: 1-942613-41-5
Library of Congress Control Number: 2016905586

First Printing: 2016
Printed in the United States of America
10 9 8 7 6 5 4 3 2 1

This publication was produced using available information.
The publisher regrets it cannot assume responsibility for errors or omissions.

Contents

Introduction

My name is Violetta Peters. I grew up in Cecilia, Kentucky, in a small community called Howevalley. My daddy owned a bulldozer, and made his living working for other people. He was also a farmer and I grew up in the tobacco fields of Kentucky. Losing my mother at an early age, I was inspired by strong devotion to write this story of recollections of my childhood, looking for momma I think, and the love she gave to us while she was living. Daddy was a strong influence on his children, and we believed in who he was. This is the part I carry with me. This is the part I'm passing on only a small portion of the story of the Hilary Peters family, and the loss of a very special lady. I'm honored to call my mother Ollie Peters.

My son Jeremy Chad Meredith and my grandson Jeremy Gage Meredith have filled my life with love and devotion. I truly believe the path of love is unending.

Dedication

Dedicated to Jeremy Chad Meredith and his son, Jeremy Gage Meredith, my grandson, my loving mother, Ollie Peters, and my daddy, Hilary Peters.

Also dedicated to my sisters and brothers, who have shared and lived the story with me:
Carolyn Goodman, Froman Peters, Vetricia Guffey, Audrey Wallace, Lecia Sanders, Duel Peters, Michael Peters.

May our lives and the story be remembered in the roots of our family.

Our trials and disappointments bear witness to them, the importance of a bond between a family.

Let love be grounded in our pathway with roots that grow beyond our trials and disappointments, and let love leave a lasting bond.

Old Black Rocking Chair

Recollections and Poems

Duel Peters, Violetta Peters, Audrey Wallace, and Tricia Guffey

Lecia Sanders and Carolyn Goodman

Section 1

Old Black Rocking Chair

Old Black Rocking Chair

The woods watch us in the summertime like thousands of eyes that jump when we jump, and run when we run.

Echoes fill the holler and linger in the vines. It is those echoes that I hear in my mind.

Counting the years in a time long ago, just turning four years old. I'm little sister.

An old dirt road leads to our front door. I guess you could say we are poor.

Carolyn, Froman, Lecia, Tricia, and Audrey are all in school. Duel and I meet them at the end of the road. My feet are muddy from the walk. I don't have any shoes to wear.

Our house is small, but we are happy.

When Momma comes home from the hospital there will be one more kid to a room.

Lights are shining through the window. Momma, Momma is home. In her arms she is carrying my new baby brother, Michael Dean. Tricia and Audrey start singing a song. We all join in and sing along.

"Hey Mike…Mike…Mike, and you Mike…Mike…Mike." He just smiles at us like he knows who we are. He never seems to cry, like he is in his own little Heaven.

It's a good thing, I guess. Momma would never get anything done. Duel is at Momma's dress strings all the time. Rubbing his eyes with tears rolling down his face. I'm afraid he is going to rub his eyes out one day if he does not stop doing that.

Momma told him, before long you will have someone to play with. Michael will be at your feet wherever you go, and the two of you will always be busy keeping up with the other.

Just a simple family. Getting by every day on simple things. Necessities that made our lives complete.

Living with Daddy, I always felt like I was more. More than a little girl with dirt on the bottom of my feet, playing outside barefoot in the summertime.

Daddy cut wood all day, and I heard him tell Momma that he just felt like he was going nowhere, but I can't imagine Daddy going nowhere.

The year has passed in this small house. Daddy says, "This house is too small for all of us."

The year is December 1961.

The fire from the wood stove has warmed every room.

Beans are cooking on the stove. Momma is sewing in the other room.

Our house sets back in the woods, and snow has covered the ground as far as you can see. Momma says, "In spots there are snow drifts over my head."

In Kentucky the woods can go on and on, if you are a country girl. Froman and Lecia have picked out a Christmas tree. Daddy's outside chopping it down.

Froman is dragging the tree through the back door. Carolyn and Lecia are behind him, cleaning up the mess Froman is leaving behind. Momma's in the attic getting boxes of Christmas ornaments down.

The smell of cedar is in the air.

I don't know what I want for Christmas, and I don't know if I believe that Santa Claus brings presents to children on Christmas Eve.

Maybe Santa Claus won't be able to find us, and we will be the only house Santa Claus doesn't see.

Momma is popping popcorn and making ice tea.

Froman is outside turning the antenna, trying to get a clear picture on TV. The rest of us are decorating the tree.

Anxiously waiting what really happens on Christmas day.

Nights have fallen and days have passed, and if Santa is coming he will be here tonight.

Toys…toys are under our tree. Something for all of us, and a baby doll for me. Duel is pushing his tractor around on the floor. Audrey and Tricia got two big desks. I have never seen anything like that.

So, there is Christmas, and Santa Claus.

One time a year he visits us all.

Life can be a veil sometimes that covers our face, then opens our eyes.

A journey into a world unknown.

My subconscious mind always wanting to go back home, to fix things undone, to kiss momma good-bye.

⌘

The woods are quietened by the cold, although the snow has melted outside and left us with a beautiful winter day.

A perfect day to go on an adventure.

Mill Holler Cave is not far from our house. A place we have talked about, but never seen. Froman has been back there with Daddy before. Daddy has walked through those woods many times.

Momma wants to go, she has never seen a cave before, and "we may never have another opportunity to," she said.

I put socks on my hands for gloves. Momma is taking Duel and me. Tricia is staying behind with Mike while Audrey runs out the door after Carolyn and Lecia. The walk was full of anticipation.

Froman, Carolyn and Lecia ran ahead, and were out of sight by the time we caught up. They were looking down on us from the mouth of the cave.

Momma's voice was frightened, "Stop, don't go any farther, this is enough." Momma never walked any closer, nor did we. Standing in eyesight, we waited for them to come down.

The cave seemed to set back in the holler, and Momma was frightened looking up at them.

Our footsteps were light walking home, as though we had really been on a far away journey.

Momma was out of breath it seemed, picking Duel up and holding him in her lap.

"What a day we have had. Don't you kids ever go there again, now remember that." I vaguely do remember this day, but in my mind a picture was taken, and looking into the entrance of Mill Holler Cave has remained in my memory like time stood still, and mystery left the door open for me to walk through some day.

Later, we heard stories about Mill Holler Cave. One was about a man who went far inside and never came out again.

They say his body is buried between the rocks of Mill Holler Cave.

Momma's been sewing all day; we all get new clothes for Easter. My dress is the one with yellow ducks on it. Material is scattered all over one side of the room.

I'm watching Michael play on the floor. The sewing machine is buzzing while Momma's talking. She tells me things when no one is around. Maybe because she thinks I'm too small to really be listening, or maybe because she knows that I am.

Daddy is bulldozing outside. He has made a short road through the woods. Several trees have been knocked down. I'm watching him through the window.

Momma said, "We all need to look after one another. I can't be everywhere all the time."

The next day Duel and I were playing in the bulldozer tracks Daddy had left behind. I fell down a small hill and got my arm caught in a tree root that had been pulled from the ground by the bulldozer. It hurt bad. I ran to the house. It's messed up bad, I think. Daddy said, "Take her to the hospital. I never broke anything. The Doctor set it, and put it in a sling.

He told me to take care of it, and I will.

I love my Momma and my Daddy.

Easter came way too soon. Momma just got finished with our dresses last night.

We don't have a camera. Aunt Avanal, Momma's sister, took our picture when we got to church. "Cute as buttons," she said. We call Aunt Avanal, "Sister". Her husband is Uncle Marrion.

He calls me bird eye, but I don't know where he got that from. I guess he thinks my eyes look like a bird.

Driving home from church, Daddy told us we were moving. He has bought a farm just off Highway 86, just a few miles from Howevalley School. "The house is big," he says, "and it will take some getting used to. You kids will be sleeping upstairs, and that will be a big change. There is no bathroom, but I'm putting one in as soon as possible under the staircase. That area is plenty big enough for a bathroom.

"I have boxes for each one of you to put your personal things in, so let's get packing! That will take care of your things.

"Momma and I can start moving while you are in school.

"Your Uncle Louie is going to help us. He is a strong guy, and ready to go."

I woke up this morning to furniture being moved out of the living room, and Uncle Louie's voice saying, "Hilary, pick it up on the other end."

When I got out of bed, the trucks were loaded down.

Daddy said, "Violetta, you and Duel come with me, your Mom's cleaning up our new house.

Duel and me were crunched together, along with as many boxes as Dad could get in the truck.

Daddy is anxious the road doesn't move fast enough in front of him.

This house is beautiful.

The rooms are so big. I can't believe we are moving in here.

Our bedroom furniture is all in place.

Kids rule upstairs.

Daddy gave Momma a big kiss when we came through the door.

Feeling like he had more than he could ever ask for.

The last piece of furniture to set into place was an old black rocking chair Momma seemed to cherish.

A corner stairway leads up to our bedroom, like a hidden passageway. Another stairway leads up the side of the wall of Momma and Daddy's room. This is a beautiful stairway. Under these steps and in this room, Daddy will put the bathroom. Everything about this place holds such change as though the world were evolving and we are caught between the tide.

Froman has a new job. He has to milk the cow every afternoon. Duel and I stood over him to watch, and he lifted the cow's teat and sprayed us with milk. We took the hint and left him to himself.

Crops are growing in the field, and I can tell Daddy is encouraged about his life at this point. Plans for a bathroom are in motion. Momma is so looking forward to that, and Daddy keeps assuring her that it won't be very long, but Momma is not feeling well, and Daddy knows something is wrong. With all the work that needs to be done, he cannot imagine other obstacles more prudent than today.

He is spread about as far as one man can be spread, but there is no time to stop, not until the day is through.

Momma is sleeping, and the house is still without her footsteps to warm the rooms. Momma has a weak heart, the doctor says. Michael's birth only weakened it more.

Momma was not supposed to have any more children, but in the '60s, life was different; children were not planned, but given, and motherhood was a cherished part of living.

Daddy is cleaning up; he is taking Momma to the hospital where she can get better.

Deep roots were planted here, and even now I know I will always remember this house, these rooms, my family, just as they are today.

The morning has awakened us with our uncle standing in the stairway. His voice is kind, but shaken as he says, "Your mother is no longer with us." What does he mean? My thoughts numb, the hour, the day, no more a memory for days and hours spin with time and destiny, ceasing to be reminded of a woman I once knew living in the shadow of my heart. Daddy was in and out of the house, not really saying very much.

The house is filled with shadows on the wall, each one leaving nothing behind. The days faded and we each found our places in the faces of one another. It was here I found myself running up the steps where time left an empty place in my heart.

Sitting on the floor staring out a window looking for something I could not find.

How could I have known that many years down the road I would look through that window again.

Dear Diary:

I know I'm only six years old, but I have a lot of things to say; things I have been holding in for years, as I walk down a road between yesterday and today. Vaguely I remember Mother combing my hair, and the shadow of an old black rocking chair. I never asked any questions, or stopped to say good-bye, and today's tears are the first I have ever cried.

Thirty-five years old… guess it's better late than never… tear drops on my face, my thoughts directed toward Heaven.

Momma's last words were weak, because I know that she was tired.

Yet they were eternal, putting all her trust in God.

Lord, my soul is ready for this journey I must take, but my time is short and there is so much for me to do. My children, one by one, as their faces leave my hands; Father, please don't forsake me, always remember.

Ollie Peters is not a big name in this community, but people came from miles around to pay their respects.

A black hearse pulled up to the back door of that old two-story house. Sad faces wheeled the casket across the kitchen floor, straight through the doors of a huge bedroom… Mom and Dad's room.

Walking up to the casket, "Is this Mother really lying there?" All dressed up in lilac, guess she's ready to go away.

Sleeping in the quiet of senders golden blooms, Momma looked awfully pretty this particular day.

Someone gave me a set of white plastic beads. A necklace. I set on the stair steps, pulling them apart and snapping them together.

Whispers begin to stir, like maybe Daddy should split us up.

Duel and I watched outside as all the cars left.

People where saying things like how was Daddy going to raise eight kids on his own.

Mike, Duel, and I never went to the cemetery; family members stayed with us at home.

Daddy's sister, who lives in Louisville, wants to raise Tricia as her own; she doesn't have any children. Maybe Sister will take Audrey, or maybe me.

We heard a lot of whispers no one thought we did, but Daddy kept us all together, and I'm glad that he did. I cannot imagine my life without my family.

Daddy was our ship, without his light we could not exist; but Momma, she was our anchor, even now I can feel the pull leading me to higher ground where greater strength lies in the Lord. Hills roll across the valley like camels backs, waiting for someone to ride, and if life has any meaning I know I'll find it here. Sheltered in the light of Daddy's heart, we were home.

Carolyn is the oldest, and she has her hands full.

Daddy depends on her to take care of us when he is not at home.

Carolyn is worried about getting her driver's license. Daddy says she has to.

Already she has run into a school bus, pulling out of our drive onto the highway.

No one was hurt, but it was enough to throw her into reclusion. Lecia keeps her cheered up, encouraging her all the way. Lecia has a way about her that makes you forget that anything is a problem.

Lecia is excited about the whole venture, and she can't wait to get a license of her own.

Carolyn was born to handle responsibility, moving with all she has, and all she knows to do, while every day becomes more of a reality of so much left undone. Teenage years and many tears, and dreams of her own.

While the world keeps turning, life falls into place even at the Peters house.

That two-story house holds memories dear, memories of security even though our lives are torn.

Daddy has dreams that Grandpa Charlie never had, and by the grace of God he will find a way.

Hilary Peters held a special place in life, and there will never be another man who will ever take his place.

Looking back, I can see so many ways we were blessed. Room to roam to feel the essence of all that is simple, and clean. Though in the years that lie ahead we will be scarred with our own fears, along life's way.

My big brother Froman is a tree carver king. Froman loves someone, but I can't remember who she was.

He and our cousin Willie swim in a pond back in the field. They could not have had more fun if that pond had been Lake Cumberland.

Froman's first set of wheels were a yellow Caterpillar; all his life he has been a bulldozer man. He laughs about it now and says, "Kids today are so undecided about what they want to do with their lives. Some of them go to college for years and still don't know what they want to do. I never had a choice. Daddy told me what I would do with mine."

I never questioned it. I just moved with words that beat like drums into my heart. Froman worked so hard at such an early age. At 15 he was doing things grown men do.

Daddy could be hard on him, and sometimes I couldn't understand why dad had to be so hard, when he was just a boy, but it must have made him strong and he has always stood on his own, his heart is big, and his eyes are gentle, so God must have helped him through it.

I didn't think anything could ever shake us. We were Hilary's kids, and some how that meant something.

Daddy was busy; he had to be. We never saw a lot of him, but his influence was strong his shadow was enough to keep us safe and warm.

Mike is like a cub bear looking for his mother under Dad's boot strings. It was no surprise to us when Daddy took him to work, and set him in a box while he ran his old bulldozer until finding a place to stop. He said Mike was no trouble, but he would never do that again. Michael always ran after Dad, crying in his footsteps, on this particular day Daddy just could not leave him behind.

There is a celebration at our house…our bathroom, our wonderful bathroom…warm baths, and no late ventures outside at night to pee.

These are good days, even though the loss of Mom will affect our lives in every way. At this time we have each other and our lives move in peaceful harmony.

My favorite place in the world is Berdenna's Store. Daddy runs a bill there every month for supplies if we need them…Coke, and bologna for sandwiches, and one cent bubble gum behind the counter. A few times the bill has gotten out of hand, leaving Dad to wonder where the money was spent, but he didn't have to wonder long…it was Lecia and our cousin, Iona, buying junk without permission.

Lecia and Iona were always bending rules, and if anybody could get away with it, it would be the two of them.

"Augh! The store!" Carolyn has left for the store. Sitting out by an old tree stump counting the cars as they drove down the road. Five more and the next one's ours; no, I think it is three.

It's Carolyn, here she comes, I see her coming down the road.

I can see Duel and Mike now counting time like it was yesterday. Chickens in the hen house gathering eggs, an old hen I thought was possessed.

Christmas at grandpa's over the hills, and through the woods. Anticipating Santa Claus as soon as we returned home. A big deal to us was staying up until 12:00, a big pan of popcorn, Elvis Presley movies. Shoot-em-up cowboy! Playing life to the rule.

Building a bar in the barn, like we seen on T.V. Sweeping our dirt floors.

Tricia sang a song I wrote, and it went like this:

"I want a man who walks. I want a man who talks. I want a man to buy me things."

I bet she doesn't remember, but I do. I didn't know it then, but in front of me somewhere a writer was yet to be found.

Lecia has a special way about her. Fourth runner-up basketball queen. A dress as beautiful as she is. Although she can be mischievous, as long as she is around there is always laughter, too.

Lecia worries more then she lets people know. Covering up her fears in the laughter of her smile. Loving each day. Sharing each moment with the kindness in her heart. Overlooking trials as though each one is recognized immediately, then set aside within herself to pass the trial on with the love that sustains her heart.

Daddy does not worry about Tricia and Audrey too much. He is satisfied in his heart that the two of them have roots that will not take them far from who they are.

Tricia is like a tree; she will not move from the illusions she has made in her heart. Already she has anchored herself in a place she feels safe and warm. The branches move, and the wind blows, but she will not be tossed to the side, anchored in the serenity of her own mind.

C❧つ

Audrey never meets a stranger; she follows her illusions like a drifting child. Her friends fall in love with her, leaving lasting bonds, though she never meets a stranger, her heart will lose anchor with her first heartbreak.

Mom dressed Tricia and Audrey like twins. They wore the same clothes, same hairdos, and even got the same toys at Christmas time, but they could never be more different Tricia and Audrey disagreeing on most everything, but finding comfort in the presence of the other. I am glad they had each other to lean on stepping stones, making memories of there own.

In later years my cousin Marchitta learned to play a piano. The three of them became a trio, singing special songs in church, their voices blended together like angels were singing.

Duel is a puzzle, hard to define; in control of everything, but himself. The world is an open door. A door he is not afraid to walk through on his own, and if it leads him down a road that's wrong, he will ride the tide until the end, then pay the debt that is due, and live to love again.

Mike was Daddy's little boy. When he was too big to carry, Daddy picked him up inside his heart.

Duel and Mike were like Indians on the run, different personalities both fighting to be free. They took more chances than me, and I was always thinking, "Please don't climb so high, don't get too close to the edge, move back a little bit. I'm afraid that you might fall."

We were the last three, us and the black birds flying over our heads, pecking the wind beneath our feet. Tucked inside angel wings, go to sleep, sleepy head. Looking back I think we were running the same race, just at a different pace. A battle of innocence, displaying our defense.

❦

Daddy's building a new house; he says it won't be cold in the mornings anymore. We will have electric heat instead of a coal burning stove. I lie awake and dream of that.

Dirt is piled up and you can see the big white house from here. The basement is dug, and it won't be long now until we will move in. Uncle Silvin is building the house, so things will move quickly from this point.

I never thought these memories would mean so much. Daddy's roots were never far from Howevalley.

The house is pretty, but I will remember the noise downstairs, where Daddy is putting coal in the stove, and the chill on my cheeks in the morning, and Sis Carolyn working so hard to keep the house clean, giving us rules to live by, while her and Lecia washed our clothes on an old wringer washer in the kitchen.

Mike sleeps with Dad sometimes, snuggling down into the covers where he feels safe and warm.

Dad woke us in the night with a terrible nightmare that he had. He held my little brother in his arms and tore down curtains in his room, trying to escape a burning fire through the window of his room. That morning we all laughed about the ruckus in the night. Dad said, "It was so real, all I could think about was saving Michael from the flames."

Years later, when Mike was only 24, he was killed in a house that had been caught on fire. Trapped inside, he was not able to escape.

Scars from death go unnoticed, and only deepen with time. But in our hearts they are still with us if it is only in our dreams.

Dad's bulldozer tracks mire in the ground, they roll across that dirt road, and they roll across my heart.

Momma's standing at the back door, and she's calling out our names.

She says, "It's too late for crying, or standing in the rain your life is now a pathway you will leave behind.

"Fourteen grandkids that I have never seen.

"Their faith is weaker than any of you.

"You were tied by an anchor protected by the lamb.

"The weakest part of you is now a part of them.

"Faith is the absence of miracles unseen, they are all part of you and they are all part of me.

"Grandma's standing at the back door, and she's calling out your names. She says, 'Life is a pathway you will leave behind.'"

❦

Sometimes life takes us where we go, and we just follow the tide.
Never having a choice, like an arrow that flies.
A shooting star of echoes that make us come alive.
Drawing breath from the distance, and the flowing tide.

Duel Peters, Violetta Peters, Audrey Wallace, and Tricia Guffey

Ollie Peters (mommy), Hilary Peters (daddy), Aunt Avanal (sister), Uncle Marrion, and Violetta Peters (in front)

Section 2

Beautiful Day

Carolyn Goodman and Duel Peters

Duel and Mike Peters

This River

This river runs through my soul,
It breathes life to my heart, flows
   through my veins.
Captured by its roaring stream.
I run with it, move with it, feel
   the touch of the stones that lie
   in my pathway.
Still I roar, alive beneath the water,
   above the water.
Over the tree's that have fallen,
   through the many, many years.
One by one into these waters where I
   run with endless mystery, endless time,
   I run.
The current still as strong as it ever was.

My Prayer

© 2016 Violetta Peters

Watch over my babies, Lord, while they sleep.
Wrap them in your perfect love.
Show them kindness like velvet skies.
May darkness close willowed eyes.
May I not live my life in vain.
For vanity hides in winds of pain.
Cast not my prayer beneath thy feet.
Let forgiveness grace the path of
    Heaven, and tonight my prayer be
    eternal.

Best Friends

© 2016 Violetta Peters

Star Wars
Camping buddies
Cigarettes
Blood brothers
Lessons learned, no stones unturned,
    Broken hearts from empty lovers,
    Hidden roads, new found dreams,
I smile to think though our lives have
    changed, in our hearts we will remain
    friends.

Chicken Coop

© 2016 Violetta Peters

A two-story house,
A two-story barn.
A chicken coop
   down on the farm.
Feather's fly up
   in the air.
Drinking life from
   a paper cup.
Setting on a roosting
   pole, waiting for the
   day to unfold.

Sisters and Brothers

© 2016 Violetta Peters

Our future is a wind blown path.
A barefoot parade of dusty tracks.
Mimic what I say, and do.
Tomorrow will be your future, too.

Freckled Wind

Happiness is a freckled wind.
    If there it could begin.
There is no innocence in the
    rain, or the fragrance of a
    frosty day.
I put a soup bone in the pot.
    Pushed some crackers into a box.
Moving with the swaying chimes.
    Tic toc, tic toc.

Jeremy Gage Meredith

God must have dropped you
    from Heaven, little snow flake,
    little star, borrowed from
    the wings of angels, Gage.
The raven's watched to catch
    you, but in our arms God has
    blessed us.
With a little piece of Heaven,
    Gage.
*Written for my grandson the day he
    was born, April 9, 1998*

Mr. Pretender

© 2016 Violetta Peters

Mr. Pretender, why do you do what you do?
Life goes on and you just let it slip away.
One hand on a bottle, and the other hand on your heart.
Every day's a promise that you acknowledge, then ignore,
   Mr. Pretender, why do you do what you do?

Death's Echo

© 2016 Violetta Peters

Lost boy, why do you look for answers in empty graves?
Your daddy's just another blind spot in the road.
A name on a tombstone that is cold.
Walk quietly over the mournful shadows that lie ahead.
Your Mother is the only living refuge to your soul.
She is the vine, where in death's echo I call you mine.
Walk softly on the fruit of the vine.

Daddy, Can I?

Daddy, can I go out in the rain?
I'm here to catch the thunder, watch it roll off my finger again.
Describing the beauty of the pain is never very pretty,
when your heart is struck by lightning again.
Tossing and turning to the beat of a thousand distant drums
    beneath my feet.
You would be proud to know I have survived.
Cried beneath the willow late upon my pillow again.
What a lovely day to be alive, still looking for a rainbow outside.
Now until the day I say goodbye to this world that has rocked me
    from side to side.
Daddy, can I go out in the rain?
I'm here to catch the thunder, watch it roll off my finger again.

Troubled Waters

© 2016 Violetta Peters

Praise God for life's troubled seas, for in these
  Troubled waters, I was set free.
My heart's destination is aiming for home.
  Where God's great glory outshines the sun.
Peace like a river gently flows, and sickness
  and death will never know.
Praise God for life's troubled seas, for in these
  Troubled waters, I was set free.
I'll rise to the sound of my new name, and in a
  twinkling of an eye I will be changed.
My body will then take its flight, and all that
  was earthly will simply die.
Down here I've stumbled all my life, but now my
  soul will soar on high.
Praise God for life's troubled seas, for in these
  Troubled waters, I was set free.
Thanks to Jesus and his nail scarred hands, and
  for my life that he now holds.
I'll soar like an eagle through the skies, and all
  that was earthly will simply die.
Praise God for life's troubled seas, for in these
  Troubled waters I was set free.

Jeremy Gage Meredith

© 2016 Violetta Peters

You will always be
my special star, that
shines with me wherever
you are.

Pale Rider

© 2016 Violetta Peters

I will rescue my name, ride through the storm.
Wipe my feet on the dust.
Smile at the thorns.
I will lift my head above the gray, and upon my horse I will ride away.
My saddle of leather will cradle my soul.
Gird my loins with hidden joy.
Giddy-up! Pale Rider, hold to the reins while we jump the thorns.
I will rescue my name, ride through the storm.
Wipe my feet on the dust.
Smile at the thorns.

The Thorns

© 2016 Violetta Peters

Life makes us who we are.
Our travels make our lives complete.
He who has been tried,
Though he is chastened, so is he born.
From the Lord, great witnesses felt the thorns.
Yet to be saved, and live.
To flower among the thorns.

Lost Little Boy

© 2016 Violetta Peters

Why are you so quiet, child?
Lost little boy behind a smile.
Together are we one, but two.
Teenage mother, lonely child.
Who is to blame for bitter dreams.
Who fails to listen to quiet screams.

Dusty Tracks

© 2016 Violetta Peters

People called him a rebel in our town. Most folks called him
trouble, I called him Dad.

He worked hard, but spun his wheels. He dreamed of Harleys, and
drove old cars.

He drank whiskey instead of wine, and he never saw me most of
the time.

Momma said, "Close your eyes, and don't look back," but I was
always chasing dusty tracks.

Sleepy rivers run through my soul.

Momma, wake me up before I drown.

Violetta

Words are candles that burn eternally.
Violet
Violetta
A color
A flower
The name my mother gave me.
Who could describe the morning in the Lilac of summer?
Miles roll across the desert.
Birds sing melodies.
Hush little darlin'.
While I tell you over again.
My love is the morning, in the lilac of summer.

Son and Grandson

© 2016 Violetta Peters

The light of love makes music play.
Hands that reach for deeper things,
find their spirit yet to sing.
Far beyond the realm of love,
    planting seeds to leave behind.
In the notes were sparkling rhymes.
Where I left my name behind.
With all that love could ever bring.
Always remember my love for you.

Sisters

© 2016 Violetta Peters

Sister, because you're you
The sun is brighter than
The skies are blue.

Treasured embers always linger near.
Like your face through the years.
Embraced by mother's hand.
Sisters hold a lasting bond.
Tied beyond the realm of time.
Chasing, wanted, wasted, years.

Now I really understand why embers echo in my ear.
Embraced by sisters throughout the years.
I love you, sister, because you're you.

Sis Carolyn
her cancer 2015
her death July 2015
Love can cast a
    great shadow over you,
Then it can cast a
    great light.

We love, and miss you,
Sister.

An Orchestra Plays

© 2016 Violetta Peters

I will never fail to see,
   the meadow play a symphony.
If I listen to the view, I will keep
   pressing on. A gentle orchestra I
   hear.
Playing music through history.
My pen takes me far.
Even travel to the stars.
If I could shelter every bloom,
There would be a haven distant far,
   and a beautiful shooting star.
Hear the music! Watch it ray,
   in a city far away.
The Lights of one we have never seen,
   so I play a symphony.
All the world is history.
Coming in across the sea. Know money
   can aspire, or take the beauty from
   the stars.
Here in meadows, country blooms.
A beautiful orchestra plays.

Sandman

© 2016 Violetta Peters

Touch the smile of a child, and hold it in your hands.
Little fingers
Little nose
The sandman sleeps.
He reminds me of yesterday.

Mother's Love

© 2016 Violetta Peters

Should my eyes close in peaceful sleep, and not be opened again
    until in Heaven's city.
If one wish could be granted from God's fair realm, I would fly down
    from Heaven on
    angel's wings, and protect you from the dangers this world brings.
You wouldn't know the wings that keep you, but you would feel the
    warmth, and touch of safety.
A mother's love is one that never dies, and if it could, her love
    would reach from beyond the
    skies in some light, some miracle only God knows.
Maybe it sometimes does.

This Zoo

© 2016 Violetta Peters

I'm a monkey in this zoo.
Behind these bars I'm called a fool.
Deliberating all the facts.
Some are true.
Some are not.
A man in blue.
A man in black.
Another reason not to drink.
Outside these bars the air is free,
and my life waits for me.
Possessed by a demon's call.
Lord, please give me the strength
    to destroy this demon called
    alcohol.

Innocent

© 2016 Violetta Peters

Sweet kiss
Sweet lullaby
Momma's breath
Innocent eyes
I'm in bondage.
Invisible chains.
I'm asleep, let me dream.
The cloud's, they are fine,
   and the winds a place in time.
If I had wings I would soar the sky,
   and forever
   be innocent.

Arrows Home

© 2016 Violetta Peters

Life springs
Short wings
Angel signs
Long walks
Honest talks
Changes things
New hope
Arrows home
Sunshine.

Celestial Sounds

© 2016 Violetta Peters

Trees can't be counted.
There are too many to call.
Leaves can't be counted.
There are too many to fall.
My love for you bares no number, none can be edified.
As light as a smile.
Like feathers that fly.
Celestial sounds, my heart's a lullaby.
When I close my eyes, they dance in the moonlight.
Closer than dreams, but can't be explained.
Love is a season, our lives embrace our love.

Beautiful Day

© 2016 Violetta Peters

A drink is one drink away.
A moment another hour of the day.
Born into this shadow.
Imprisoned by chains.
I vowed to never take another
    drink.
Outside the woods are green.
An angel whispered to me.
What a beautiful day to be
    free.

Violetta, Lecia, Froman, and Mike

Section 3

Freedom

Jeremy Chad Merdith (son)

Southern Bells

© 2016 Violetta Peters

Southern winds of beauty ray, split the sky like purple hay.
Then in fields of distant drums, dance the shadows of Indian maids.
In the echoes of the wind, I heard the cries of southern bells.
Oh, Kentucky! Oh, Kentucky! Where I ran, where I played,
   where I fought the battles of
   yesterday.
Lay me down in the sun, lay me down where shadows run.
I cried until I could not cry.
I laughed until I could not laugh, and in my heart the thunder rolled.
Oh, Kentucky! Oh, Kentucky! Where I will spend my dying days
   looking for those distant
   rays.

United We Stand

© 2016 Violetta Peters

Lord, we are a nation built on love,
But if we need to fight, please be our
Shield and guiding light.
Please grant our soldiers abiding
Strength to protect them from our
Enemy's hand.
   For spacious skies
   Red, white and blue
   Let freedom ring, America.
   Cannons fired long ago.
   Distant bullets
   Desert Storm
   Jungle movements in the rain
   Battleships
   Dropping bombs
   World War I
   World War II
   Vietnam
Our greatest power lies in God
United we stand, America.

Indian Reservation

© 2016 Violetta Peters

The world is our anchor.
The universe our guide.
Every creature tells a story
  of many, many tribes.
Indian echoes in the distance.
Herding winds of buffalo.
Dancing in the realm between
  heaven and the earth.
Our spirits will gather, and
  our name will be the wind.
Riding on the thunder of white
  buffalo.

Lost Soldier

© 2016 Violetta Peters

Evening comes, evening falls.
In the sun, in the moonlight.
In the darkest hour of my life.
Gentlemen, gentlemen
I'm a mountain.
I'm a hurricane.
I'm a lost soldier searching for my wings.
In the sun.
In the moonlight.
In the darkest hour of my life.

© 2016 Violetta Peters

Living in a day when our country is being sold.
Leaving us hopeless aspirations.
Watching history unfold.
Stung by a bullet piercing our souls.
He wears a face disguised by man.
He wears a number, not a name.
He is yet.
Our strength is love.
Our hope, and aspirations lie above.

Angels and Men

© 2016 Violetta Peters

War has no boundaries, but crosses all lines to defend and defeat.
Victory rises above the cannons, while death chooses sides.
Bombs leave no one captive, only the smoke that fills the sky.
Freedom is worth dying for.
There is no price too high.
If we could mend broken arrows now shot to defend.
See through the eyes of war.
Conquer the need for battles now shattered in defense.
Our lives no more set by boundaries of men.
Precious is the gift to breathe, and feel the pain.
Soldiers in a battle of angels and men.

Indian Brave

© 2016 Violetta Peters

My people live in walls thin and bare.
Our names picked from the spirits of birth.
Every creature wears the beauty of this earth.
Not a red, but a pale Indian brave lies in the shadows of yesterday.
Pressing my ear to the ground.
I can hear the thunder of a thousand buffalo.
Living our lives to be swallowed by the land.
My people now an emblem, not a tribe.
White eagles spread their wings to fly.
While they take the songs from the bird's in the sky.
Captured by many roaring streams, looking for a vision that never came.
Camping around the fire, brave Indian warriors proclaim.
We where here before the white man came, and took our visions from the flame.

Wings

© 2016 Violetta Peters

Spread your wings, mighty eagle.
Feel the air beneath our feet.
Bird of our nation,
Symbolizing we are free.

Israel

© 2016 Violetta Peters

I love to interpret my dreams.
When crystal waters rise, I see.
I'm a drifting shadow in the night.
In a land where mighty men knew my name.
I'm not quite the land I used to be.
Now I wear a face called yesterday.
Where in silent castles kings were
thrown, and promises were made to men.
Here I hold a place in time sand, and
   wind have not brushed away, and tears
   from a troubled land.
Where a queen was taken in the night.
Her face was wrapped in linen so tight,
   and from the depth of all eternity it
   was the face of Israel that I had seen.

Chastened Dream

© 2016 Violetta Peters

Chastened by a dream, Abraham Lincoln soared to reach his destiny.
President of the United States.
He lived his life to set others free.
Looking to justify the soul of men.
He saw no race, or color of skin.
His heart touched, and so did rend.
Freedom for everyone.

Abraham Lincoln

© 2016 Violetta Peters

An old Indian taught me to see through the eyes of nature.
Moving with the river and the expectations that lie ahead.
Oars vexed against my chest.
Running with a fever.
Burning through my soul.
In these days of providence, wanton with desire.
I'm Abraham Lincoln, raging spirit, captive by the waters.

America

© 2016 Violetta Peters

In gallant waves across the sky.
In realms of yesterday.
America, America, God give us grace today, and crown thy
    word with brotherhood, throughout our lives today.
America, America, the words in beauty ray.
Let freedom ring, red, white and blue, for spacious skies
    we pray.
America, America, sweet home of liberty, and crown thy word
    with brotherhood throughout our lives today.
In gallant waves across the sky, In realms of yesterday.
America, America, the words in beauty ray.

Freedom

© 2016 Violetta Peters

As I live, so shall I die.
My sword as my lantern.
A shield to light.
Let us sleep.
Let us dream.
Let us arm ourselves with peace, and love.
I stand on a bridge.
The bounty of deliverance.
I will fight with the peasants and reign with the kings.
I'm freedom.
Those who have fought against evil.
Laid down our lives for peace.

Strong as a Lion

© 2016 Violetta Peters

I will be strong as a lion.
Think as many.
Draw my strength from love.
Overcome the evil tempter,
    witness the taste of victory
    in my soul, bite the taste of death.
More valuable than myself, love
My sword a lamb.
My voice will cry above the thunder.
I will murder you. Put you in the
    flames, back into the darkness where
    you came.
My mind will rest, for I have slain the
    mighty dragon with my sword of love.

Spilling Innocence

© 2016 Violetta Peters

Compelling beast.
Dragon's tongue.
Drink the blood of innocence.
Footsteps drape eternity.
Casting lots upon my heart.
Perfume spilled like sweet sunsets.
Burn the twilight with its tongue.
Spilling blood of innocence.

Summer's Spoken Blue

© 2016 Violetta Peters

Maybe it was summer's frozen rain
That made me miss you so much.
Miss your kiss.
Miss your touch.
If not for summer's spoken blue,
    Summers empty shade of you.
Count the memories on the wall.
One by one, watch them fall.
That's when I think of you, and
    Summer's empty shade of blue.

Ageless Beauty

© 2016 Violetta Peters

Words are beauty.
So I write.
Misunderstood by so many
　　in my life.
Growing up in a back street town.
When all it's ever done was put me
　　down.
Beneath the scales of drifting tides.
Past the sunset's gliding skies.
In the wind tunnels hail.
Drifting down upon my head tonight.
Lightning strikes, thunder rolls,
And in the end it all surpasses me.
Ageless beauty going under.
Trying hard to beat the thunder.
While my heart's on a one way street.
Misunderstood by so many
　　as it beats.
Beneath the scales of drifting tides
Past the sunset's gliding skies.
In the wind tunnels hail drifting down
Upon my head tonight.

Stethoscope of Love

50 Years Together – Miss You!

This stethoscope reminds me, I'm alive.
A stethoscope of memories, beating from
   my heart.
50 years together, and each day seems
   brand new.
Flowing from my mind like echos that
   I knew.
Now I'm riding with the wind.
Counting pictures on the wall.
With this stethoscope of love.
Beating from my heart.

Jeremy Gage Meredith
(grandson)

Jeremy Gage Meredith (grandson)

Section 4

Spinning Wheels

Carolyn, Froman, Lecia, Audrey, Tricia, Duel, and Violetta

Mike Peters

Answer

I guess it's really true what they say.
Ain't love funny.
Ain't love strange.
You think you find the answer
    then it rains.

Survive

© 2016 Violetta Peters

No iron bars on my cell
Or steel doors to close.
Yet I'm locked inside
   a prisoner of my life
   always occupied trying
   to survive.

Wind Chimes

Sleep while wind
chime's weep, but
if wind chimes
weep,
how can I sleep?

Spinning Wheels

© 2016 Violetta Peters

He drinks moonshine from an old tin cup,
    calls my name like I don't know what's up.
Hides his face in spinning wheels.
Where my heart is taken by his will.
That hides my face in spinning wheels.

Love Melody

© 2016 Violetta Peters

If all music played the same melody.
Then no broken heart could ever be free.
If our love is bound to fade.
Bound to drift away.
I cannot hide beneath the tide while this ship sails away.
Old love songs are ageless.
They never die.
Just wait by the river for someone to cry.

Running Cloud

© 2016 Violetta Peters

Sheena was his only love, pale water flows like a dove.
By the river of the mountain he can hear her
call his name.
Running Cloud, Running Cloud echoing senders from a
bleeding Cherokee.
Tribal chiefs understood, and beat the drums for his
pain. Called him a valley of spirits where troubled
souls search their dreams. Gave him feathers from
the river to wear in his hair, and beads from the
mountains to scout a warrior's dreams. There he rode
the trails of thunder as freely as his name.
Running Cloud, Running Cloud, echoing senders from a
bleeding Cherokee.
Can I not be the breath you breathe? Can my breath
not be all you need? Can I not whisper to the sea,
bring her love back to me?
Sheena was his only love, pale water flows like a dove
By the river of the mountain he can hear her call his
name.
Running Cloud, Running Cloud.

Spider's Web

© 2016 Violetta Peters

His cup was empty except for
  a spider's web.
Where the widow laid her eggs.
There the spider scurried in a
   rush, and held the widow captive
   by the spinning of his web and
   the venom of her touch.

Write a Song

© 2016 Violetta Peters

Write a song, build a dream on paper.
It's so easy to find love that never
    leaves you blue on paper.
With pencil in my hand I'll draw the
    perfect plan on paper.
I'll write a melody so soft that it
    never leaves me lost on paper.
In some hidden fantasy we'll ride
    off in our dreams on paper.
Then both of us will know love was
    always ours to hold on paper.
No one wants to care, and no
    one wants to share and no one wants
    to believe love is there, and the wind
    blows so cold when the only love you
    hold's on paper.
Write a song, build a dream on paper.

Boundaries

© 2016 Violetta Peters

I cannot love you.
Though you are my love.
Though you are fair.
Rare are the moments that cease the hours.
Caught within the boundaries of our hearts.
Defying time.
Though I walk through a candlestick.
Tip toe through the water now touching my feet.
Age has no boundaries on our love,
if in our hearts we are free.
So shall our love wash upon the sands of destiny,
caught within the boundaries of our hearts.

Dreams

You haunt me like some dream.
I can't get over, and I can't get through.
So tonight when I dream.
I will dream of you.

Your Memory

© 2016 Violetta Peters

Can you hear me?
Can you hear me call your name?
In the corner of my memory where you stay.
In the silence of my dreams, I set in doubt.
Wondering if there were some way out.
Locked inside your memory.
I will always be with you.
A part of the air you breathe.
A part of your memory.

Untouched by Time

This waters cold.
The current rolls on like a river
    road.
My tongue mystified.
Words just can't describe.
How beautiful this river flows.
Old trees spiral through the banks,
running deep, dancing in history.
Where I feel like they are a part
    of me.
Waving their echo's through my
    mind.
Decade's of mystery.
Washing their branches with me.
A rage, a force of time captivated
    by life.
A roaring stream, flowing through
    the earth.
Divine, untouched by time.

Neon Blue

© 2016 Violetta Peters

This sea covers me.
I cannot breathe for the grasp of the tide
Falling deeper into your eyes that
    follow me.
Captured by moments spent in your
    arms.
Holding to your touch as days go by.
I have seen a sparrow's wings so delicately
    spawned by the light.
She cannot move.
She cannot fly
Without the blue in
    her sky.

Two Hearts

Together our thoughts shall compromise.
I will give you my body, my love.
Our dreams as one.
I will lie with you.
Your flesh as mine.
Two hearts.
One rhythm in time.

Little Fish

© 2016 Violetta Peters

You are a shark, and I a fish.
Swallowed by your body.
Fighting to be free.
You realize I lie in the stomach
    of your will.
Consumed by a fire a prisoner of
    these walls, where my heart is
    empty with desire.
One day I will find the strength
    to escape the capture of your
    kiss, and in your heart you will
    miss the love from this little
    Fish.

Red Winged Summer

© 2016 Violetta Peters

Red Winged Summer.
Soft skies of blue.
Leave winter snowflakes in the air.
Falling from the countryside, over
    hills, and valleys wide.
Into the summer a black bird flies.
Leaving winter shadows fall,
A red winged summer lingers here.

Venom

Venom on your lips
   cursed the day we met
   Evil all around, but
   I never heard a sound.
Crushed by the silence
   my virgin womb will cry.
How will I save tomorrow
   when blindness fills my
   eyes.

When the Sun and Moon Collide

© 2016 Violetta Peters

The road to love can be a long,
   long road.
It can be a willow, or a vine.
Harvest the sun, and it will
   burn inside.
Leave your heart wondering why.
Play with the moon, and lose control.
Leaving heartache in your soul.
Passing moments render near.
Love is gold.
Precious is the casting vine, that
   you hold in your mind.
Sweet, no doubting ties.
When the sun and moon collide.

Broken Love

© 2016 Violetta Peters

I fall to sleep.
I close my eyes.
My breath is love.
Yours is lies.
I will remember your
    memory.
I'll take you with me
    where I go.
Truth is strong, it bears
    the tide.
Rolling in across the sea,
    and in the fall, and winter's
    end.
It always comes back again.

Rainbows

© 2016 Violetta Peters

There are many shades of sunshine.
Some hidden in the rain.
Many colors of a rainbow translucent
gleaming beams.
I sat upon the thunder, looking for a
star.
Surrounded by the gravity of my own
beating heart.
There has to be a rainbow, but it seems
so far away.
Together we can reach it if it doesn't
slip away.

Broken Candles

© 2016 Violetta Peters

Broken candles
Broken dreams
Misplaced sandals
Runaway train
Over the river
Through the woods.
Love lies waiting.
Understood
Drifting slowly.
Where shadows fall.
In the darkness know
One sees at all.
Broken candles
Broken dreams
Misplaced sandals
Runaway train.

Nowhere

He walked down the road, nowhere.
He walked down the road, nowhere,
    and I said, "Baby, oh baby! Where
    are you going?"
He said, "I'm going down the road,
    nowhere."

Riding on a Star

© 2016 Violetta Peters

Catch a ride, it don't cost nothin'.
Baby, I really thing you're something.
We could go far riding on this star.
Where love breaks the hour.
Soft as pedals from a flower.
Past the midnight quiet embers,
    that leave you empty when you surrender.
Baby, we could go far riding on this
    star.

Little Maid

A high-minded man could be free, but his spirit
   is held by the wind.
Behind every story lies the truth.
I would not want to be a stone, or the doormat
   people walk on.
A caterpillar turns into a butterfly.
The northern star never moves in the sky.
Once I was a little maid, my pennies were
   spent, and paid.
A child runs through the rain.
Goodnight sweet kiss of fate.
Sleep is a heavenly sound, if there you find
   peace and love.

This Kiss

Icicles hanging from the trees.
A town frozen in time as far as
   I can see.
Never another moment like this.
In the chill of this hour can
   you catch this kiss.

Puppet

Who am I?
Am I a fly?
   or a Puppet
   dangling from
   a string.
Is this my future?
   or my past, or
   just another windblown
   path.

Hourglass

© 2016 Violetta Peters

Touch the night, freeze
the moment.
Lie with me on an
island of sand.
Love is an hourglass.

Elegant Swan

The sea is beautiful every hour
of the day.
In his arms I'm his flower, his
bouquet.
Here love drifts across a lake
of elegant swan.

I knew a man who lived on a
    mountain.
He gazed at the stars with mud in
    his eyes.
Hidden in the dark, he cried.
I cried, and then he laughed
    like a clown with mud in his eyes.

Thirsty Dawn

© 2016 Violetta Peters

Hours spin where time does fall.
Waking up to winter's call.
Colors fade like wicked tongues
    that scream at you when they are done.
Leaving branches, naked, bare.
Breathless beauty everywhere.
Stalking shadows cast their spell.
Halloween is in the air.
Tangled web, lovers spawn.
Breathe upon a thirsty dawn.
Finely woven with their tongue.
Two hearts beating into one.

Two Stars

© 2016 Violetta Peters

They fell from the sky
   two stars
1 night
1 love
1 light.

Until I'm Free

© 2016 Jeremy Chad Meredith

Used with permission.

The moon and stars are shining down.
God's angel's wings are all around.
Draped with stairs that seem so near.
Oh! How I miss, and love you dear.
Under the moon and stars I sit, and pray.
Hoping we will find each other someday.
Angel's wings protect me.
Keeping me safe until I'm free.

Made For Me

© 2016 Violetta Peters

Somewhere there is an easy avenue.
Simplifying all the doubts, and
 attitudes.
Lying softly on a pillow made
 for me.

Bright Red Flower

© 2016 Violetta Peters

I see a bright red flower in my mind.
One I haven't seen in a long, long time.
Since I met you my whole world's blooming new.
A bright red flower standing true.
Each petal stands for something you, and
   I will do, a love we can share our whole
   Life through.
Let's treat the flower with love dear, so the
Petals don't die out, and let the love we
   share together last forever.
I see a bright red flower in my mind.
One I haven't seen in a long, long time.
Since I met you, my whole world's blooming
New, a bright red flower standing true.

Pumpkin Seed

© 2016 Violetta Peters

The air is chilled,
And all a fright.
I picked a pumpkin
big, and bright.
I drew a face, and
carved a grin
Told myself, my heart
would be the last cry
of a pumpkin seed.

Hilary Peters, Carolyn, Froman, Audrey, Violetta, Lecia, Duel, Tricia, and Mike

Froman

Duel

Section 5

Reflections

Fearful Cry

© 2016 Violetta Peters

The wind blew from east to west.
Angels flew over her head.
Even the ocean bellowed rage as it swallowed her last child.
One by one she dropped them from the bridge, into the setting sun.
What have you done?
In a schizophrenic rage, rocking her babies to sleep.
Can you hear the angels sing?
Then she calls their names.
The lawyer said, "She was innocent from the blood of her own hand."
Shaking his head, the judge just said, "One by one, you threw your
    children from that bridge."
Taking the lives of your three sons.
Listening to every word.
Rocking her babies to sleep.
Looking up, she replied,
"Can you hear them sing?
Three angels around God's throne?"
Then she starts to call their names.
Imprisoned by the blood of innocence.
I heard her cry.
I don't no why?

Gethsemane

There is a rose in Gethsemane's garden,
A beautiful flower left there for me.
I wanted to pick it, and take it home.
Water it gently so it wouldn't die.
The air was cold, but the sun set high on
    that beautiful flower, so it wouldn't
    die.
There is a rose in Gethsemane's garden,
A beautiful flower left there for me.

The Wait

© 2016 Violetta Peters

Saddened eyes
Walls of fear.
Hidden doors, drawing near.
Feet of thunder, but I
cannot escape.
For it's only in my mind
   the thunder quakes.
Listening eyes, watching me.
Silence screams the death
   that waits.

Step By Step

© 2016 Violetta Peters

Step by step each winding chime,
bring me closer to the day, when
life itself will slip away, and
I will stand where time stands still,
and life begins one endless day.

Greet the Day

© 2016 Violetta Peters

My body rises to greet the day,
    but it is the Lord who sets the pace.
Holds the universe in place.
If any good comes from me it is the
    master who sets me free.
Gives me strength to win this race.
Not an evening, but a morning star.
In the light of Jesus we are held
    by his love.

Some Tears

Somebody fought to be free,
  and the battle was worth it
  to me.
Somebody laughed, and I laughed,
  somebody smiled, and I smiled,
  somebody cried, and I said, "Some
  tears were meant to be shed."

Essence of a Flower

© 2016 Violetta Peters

Life is the essence of a
  flower.
Time, a grain of sand
  dwindling in the hour.
Only to find what really
  matters in the essence
  of a flower.

Spring

© 2016 Violetta Peters

Share with me the colors
   of spring.
Give me pretty flowers.
Give me rain.
Blooming arrays,
Sweetly defined,
Anxiously awaiting
Summertime.

Wounded Bird

© 2016 Violetta Peters

Wounded bird, you fly
    so high.
Don't you know, soon you
    will die.
Wounded bird, your wings
    are weak.
Your flight so high will
    end in sleep.

Scarlet Harvest

© 2016 Violetta Peters

Behold the beauty so divine
   the scarlet harvest drapes
   the vine.
Grapes of rapture
Sparkling wine.
In a vineyard lost in time.

First Breath

© 2016 Violetta Peters

God is the first breath
His beginning, the end.
His end, the beginning.

My Life is Held

© 2016 Violetta Peters

The Lord holds my life in the palm of his hands,
　　and every moment that I live is His.
By the grace and mercy of His love, in the valley
　　of forever, I will stand.
On a hill on the old rugged cross, he paved the way
　　of mercy and love.
No more to acclaim those chains
His sacrifice will forever stand.
The world stood still that day.
Though the hills of forever did ring.
Rumbling in the earth of castles and kings.
His blood pierced the soul of man.
The Lord holds my life in the palm of His
　　hands, and every moment that I live is His.
Every moment that I live is His.

Angel Dreams

© 2016 Violetta Peters

When angels dream, what do
   they see?
Through mirrors of water
   ageless in time.
Their faces shine in a
   light divine.

Crimson Tide

Spirits rise and spirits sing
   in the wings of a distant light.
Who picks flowers on a windy day,
   when the prettiest flower could
   be swept away.
In the crimson of the moon, and
   the tide.

Sleeping Dogs

© 2016 Violetta Peters

Let sleeping dogs
   run in packs,
   on distant roads
   that never come
   back.

Volcano

The ocean is not glass, but a breath of
    living water.
There lies a picture of beauty, flowers
    and serenity, soon to be consumed by a
    volcanic eruption.
He lives with us on the island of the sun,
    but today our lives were awaked by this
    enraged mountain of destruction.

Bouquet

I walked the distance of a man, and felt the weight
 of a pulling wind.
Angels fly through eternity, but I felt the chill of
 Satan's hand.
The prettiest flower, who can say.
Maybe the ones you pick for your bouquet.
Sometimes the road's been hard to find, and I prayed
 for a candlelight.
Did you ever see the grass so green, or pick the
 prettiest flower you ever seen.

One Man's Mansion

© 2016 Violetta Peters

Standing in the sun.
Watching the splendor of fall.
Ageless in time.
Defiant renown.
While in some man's mansion
    doors seem to close.
One man cried out, "It runs through
    my soul."

Free Bird

© 2016 Violetta Peters

Bird's do
Travel,
Sing,
Touch the sky,
Free.

Free

© 2016 Violetta Peters

Feeling free.
Like a bird in a
    High oak tree.
Thinking of home,
    Spreading my wings.
But a warm blanket
    holds me, and I
    dream.

Waiting

I just sit here under this tree,
    with a shadow hanging over me.
I know I'm wasting time, but I
    just sit here, waiting for the
    sun to shine.

No Road Map

© 2016 Violetta Peters

Hell's a place where mercy has passed.
A fiery furnace that burns God's wrath.
Call on His name, for He is the door.
escape the wrath of eternity's flame.
God said, "There would be a day when the
    world would end." And that
We must prepare for a home in
    Heaven.
There is no roadmap to a place called
    Hell, but by nature we grow into sin's
    pathway.
Through the love of Jesus we will answer
    when He calls.
Nothing but pure will enter gates of gold.
Mercy holds life eternal, and God is the roadmap
    past a fiery furnace.
Life is short and the time is nigh.
Ring the door where glory shines.
Peace will seal your blood's lost fate, and
    that peace will carry you into the gates of
    Heaven.

The Other Side

© 2016 Violetta Peters

There would be no bad if everything was bad.
There would be no good if everything was good.
Sin lies within us all, but evil is another's call.
A perfect place would be called Heaven.
A place where no sin dwells, and good is
    not a word that could describe what
    waits for us on the other side.

Our Leader

© 2016 Violetta Peters

God is our leader, and we are
   His sheep.
I'll follow the star.
   for He is the light.
Only in Him can I start
   to begin.

A Friend

© 2016 Violetta Peters

Smile when you can
Even when you don't
    understand.
Show kindness, people matter.
The way they think.
The way they feel.
Few are losers in this
    world.
Most people just need a hand
Smile when you can.
Show the world you are a friend.

Locked Inside

I watched a movie years ago, about a man
   locked inside himself.
Describing details would be more a story
   than a rhyme.
Looking inside his pain ridden eyes, and
   the empathy I felt.
If a man were locked inside himself.

Peaceful Water

© 2016 Violetta Peters

The woods sound spooky when the sun goes down.
That's when my backyard lights up with night
    sounds.
I don't believe in ghosts, or graves that hold bad
    things, but when I was young I used to think about
    those things.
I do believe in solemn harbors where death is pronounced
    by God's great hand, and all who live will live again.
Let me walk down a path where crickets sing, and
    children laugh.
Let me pray for peaceful water, and lovely shades of
    summertime.

Stallions

Horses road the wind and owned the land.
In herds of thunder, wild and free.
Stallions of brilliant ecstasy.
Possessed by the wind, wild and free.

Play Me a Pretty Song

© 2016 Violetta Peters

I believe in sweet sunsets.
I believe in nursery rhymes.
Play my heart a pretty song, and
   I'll be there to sing along.
You and me, now that's a tune. Just
   the kind that never fades.
Through my heart like winter chimes.
Melting in the sweet sunshine.
I'll be there to dry your tears.
I'll be there to calm your fears.
The two of us are far and near.
The two of us are right on time.
Play me a pretty song, and I'll be
there to sing along. The two of us,
   you, and me.

Always and Forever

© 2016 Violetta Peters

From Christ rose many rivers.
The rivers were man and in the
    rivers he wrote his name.
Always and forever.
I will come again, and from these
    Rivers life will ever flow.
Always and forever.
A-Men

Traveling Pilgrim

© 2016 Violetta Peters

Traveling pilgrim, our footsteps are marked.
By ages and ages cut from the vine.
Passing in floral, luminous blue, embers
    still linger inside my heart.
They roll with the sunsets then with the dew.
Ages, and ages bend from the vine.
Just a few days, so little time.
Marked by the sunsets, then by the dew.
Voices of love cut from the vine.
    to gather the flowers passing through
    time.

Riverside

© 2016 Violetta Peters

Waking up to find the summer.
Resting near a riverside.
While a snow bank in December drifts
    across a winter sky.
Skating on a frozen pond.
Icicles hanging from a barn.
A narrow path that leads me home.
Waking up to find the summer.
Resting near a riverside.

Splendid Rhymes

© 2016 Violetta Peters

Echoes fall like splendid rhymes.
That break the silence in my mind.
Kentucky winds, pearl, the day.
Steal the quiet nestled bloom.
Soar the skies like rippling tides.
In these meadows time arrays.
Weaving shadows, seasons run.
Harbor near a kindred vine.
Rolling hills, bliss the sun.
With youthful shades of summer time.
Fields that make my heart aspire.
Love, and hope grow here in the land I love.
Oh, Kentucky! Oh, Kentucky! In your soil
I wrote my name.

Rocks of Beauty

© 2016 Violetta Peters

There is beauty in the rocks
   in the sand.
In the days of yesterday.
In a time far away
   existing till today.
   till today is yesterday,
   and tomorrow drifting vines,
   that spiral in time.
I love the sky.
The moon, the sun.
Yes He was the drifting sand, and
   He stood among the light,
   He was the light, He is the light.
Just as He was in yesterday.
He has not changed today.
The plan of God great creator,
   He is time.
Extending from beyond.
Naturally abiding forever.
He is love.

Butterfly

How do you catch a butterfly?
Who are you to try?
Let it spread its
   pretty wings and fly.

Purple Butterfly

© 2016 Violetta Peters

Familiar faces watched her laugh.
Familiar faces watched her cry.
Then I looked outside my window,
    at a purple butterfly.
Reality's a ladder that reaches
    toward the sky.
Put your hands on the four winds,
    just to see if you can fly.
It was the secrets of a young girl,
    with ribbons in her hair, and the
    stories of the four winds, that she
    carried in her heart.

Luminous Color

© 2016 Violetta Peters

I borrowed the night, and the night was a million stars.
God painted the sky with luminous color.
Sleep for in the days of kings there were rulers of men.
Interpreters of dreams.
Jesus turned the dead into the living, and water into wine.
I will look passed the night, past a million luminous stars
    to the throne of grace.

Reflections

© 2016 Violetta Peters

Walking through my field out back.
I could hear the footsteps of Indian maids.
Washing their clothes in the river.
Looking through the water as if it were a mirror.
Over my shoulder I heard a splash.
A tribal Indian from the past.
Gently he moved across the water as his spirit reflected
    the beauty of the forest.
His footsteps faint, but I could hear them oh so plain.
I shivered in the sun, just to see how far I had come.
Gazing into the trickling creek overwhelmed by this
    intrusion, from nature, and all its wonderful illusions.
In a place where centuries are merely paths through time.
Reflections someone else will leave behind.

Survive

© 2016 Violetta Peters

No iron bars on my cell
Or steel doors to close.
Yet I'm locked inside
    a prisoner of my life
    always occupied, trying to
    survive.

A Reminder

Sunlight guides the path that's right,
    when morning hours seem so bright.
Dark shadows pass away, and Heaven's mercy awakens
    a brighter day.
I need not forget days of gloom. When darkness
    walked in empty rooms.
A reminder of how life can change, and empty
    rooms can be filled with sunshine.

Dust of the Land

© 2016 Violetta Peters

Surely this land is holy.
Surely it is blessed.
If from the dust of the earth God created man.
Then the pathway of life began from the dust of
    the land.
Great bodies of water, and trickling creeks,
    surround our world with endless mystery.
Endless time.
Below the water
Below the tide.
Lies the foundation of man.
God's breath spoke into existence.
    a form of life so precious to the lamb,
      not even the foundation of the world will
      hold His love.
The Lord is returning.
We are all sinners.
We must be born again.
Spiritually awakened to Holy grace eternal.
Christ our Lord.

Old Country Church

© 2016 Violetta Peters

There's an old country road, and a memory I know. Where the
sun always shines there for me.

Some day I will go where love never grows cold, and that
old country church rolls on.

There the streets are paved with gold, and the Lord owns it all.

In a place called our Heavenly home.

I'll join in the choir singing songs I've acquired. In a
place called an Old Country Church.

Amazing grace how sweet the sound. That saved the wretch like
me. I once was lost, but now I'm found.

In a church by an old country road.

Some day I will go where love never grows cold, and that old
country church rolls on.

Mystery

© 2016 Violetta Peters

In its mouth teeth, as if on its tongue a voice could speak.
This long creature wore the body of a snake.
Head held high with a dragon's face.
It spun through the water as if with pride.
By its side a slithering mate.
In their bodies bore stings like death as if in fiction
    this dream was kept.
Fast were the moves of these demons thunder, quick were
    the waves that stung the water.
If only there they stayed, but on the land they begin to gaze.
I looked for friends who once were near, but saw no trace
    of the laughs we shared.
Then in silence, I woke from a dream of mystery in slumber spoke.

Land of Pearl

© 2016 Violetta Peters

Bright colored pearls.
Footprints in snow.
Keep the peace, in ever loom.
In perfect sunset blooms.
In canyons milled in stone.
In rivers far away.
Finely woven
Golden seal
Left to seek a land of pearl.
Marching in the sun.
All sails bound for home.
Where footprints never fail,
To bring you home.

A Day to Remember

© 2016 Violetta Peters

The wind blew back my hair as I remembered
    passing hours.
Lying beneath the sun, the cool breeze blowing
    in September.
Life is like a dream.
Waking to December.
What a lovely day to remember.

Sea Shells of Rock of Ages

© 2016 Violetta Peters

Echoes lie in the bottom of a sea shell. There
    they live forever captured by the sea.
Through roaring waves of thunder tossed upon the
    sand.
Living forever as long as time shall stand.
In the book of Rock of Ages, in the beginning and
    the end.
Captured by light and roaring thunder.
The waves of life roll in like the tide, then they
    roll back again.
Our lives quickly sustained in the roaring of waves,
    and quickening thunder, and in the end there is only
    the beginning.
Whenever the tide rolls in.
Through the sea shells of Rock of Ages, in the beginning
    and the end.

Your Heart

© 2016 Violetta Peters

Take away your heart,
and lose your soul.
Take away the cut and jive,
and lose the fun in life.
Take away the moon, and
you'll never fall in love.
Take away the stars, and
your dreams will die.

Shelter

© 2016 Violetta Peters

Cover me while I run for shelter.
Underneath some shade tree.
I feel a shadow creeping up on me.
A lady crying, but it's not me.
Desperation is a desperate need.
I want to help you lift your eyes.

Southern Sky

© 2016 Violetta Peters

Sing to me,
   softly sweet,
   southern sky,
   about flowers,
   blue birds, and
   pretty butterflies.

Quiet Day

A quiet day sets in the sand, spins in the
wind, reaps the harvest of golden blooms.

Golden Hours

© 2016 Violetta Peters

Dancing with the North Wind.
I know he's keeping time.
In and out of nowhere
    is never easy as it seems.
Tip my hat to the seasons
    and golden hours of summertime.

Home

The sky is bright.
   in the sunlight,
bright as stars in
   the night.
Tranquil, silent,
   vibrantly alive.
Music plays
The sound of laughter,
   falling from the
   countryside.
Dancing in
   the breeze.
Dancing in
   the winter
   time.
It is sweet.
Sweet to
   be alive.
Sweet to
   love, laugh,
   smile.
Home is a
   seed of love
   in your heart.

Starting and Beginning

To start
To finish
To begin
To end
Air
Breath
Life
Giving
Starting and Beginning

Friends

When I think of you
   your smile, your face
The kindness in your voice
   where I found comfort from day to day.
A million questions
A million reasons why
Then I smile, I laugh, and I cry.
I smile, I laugh, and I cry.
   friends forever
   beyond time.
Beyond questions or reasons why.

Your Own Soul

© 2016 Violetta Peters

Listen to the quiet when everything is still.
The hush of silence.
Peace, be still.
The void of nothing, just the air.
Nothing to touch.
Nothing is there.
Darkness, and you're all alone.
You answer for your own soul.
You answer alone.

Quiet Senders

Instant
Quiet
Frail
Near
Bloom
Where summer cast a sweet perfume.
Hail the night, hail the wind that burns by candlelight.
Rest in peace in quiet senders of sweet perfume.

Colors of Roads

© 2016 Violetta Peters

Roads of purple.
Roads of white.
Roads deep with hazy light.
Lives laughter.
Happy faces.
Remember smiles from love's embraces.
Desperate moments.
Desperate days.
Days when roads seem dark and gray.
Time passes.
Colors change.
Beauty arrays in the darkest of storms.
Where thunder booms and lightning flashes.
In the stillness,
Overwhelming peace.

Abuse

Raise your sword through a thousand ages.
Battles of gender tear the pages.
Heaping his breath, and a dragon rages.
She sits by the fire awaiting his arrival.
Looking for wings to flee from danger.
Simple and sweet, ignoring the wavers.
Looking for strength to tear the pages that
    have rocked the world for a thousand ages.

The Call

The sting of death, life's last call.
A silent whisper no one hears at all.
Except for the body that lies so cold.
An empty face where life once flowed.
He hears the voice of the father's call.
Come with me, this brand new day.
Where angels sing, and Heaven waits.

If I Stand

If I stand I first may fall.
How can I see unless I cry.
How can I laugh unless I smile.
If I listen, then I will hear.
With all my heart.
With all I have.

© 2016 Violetta Peters

To touch something moved by lies
Paralyzed
Trapped
My feelings
Immobilized
Nothing
Numb

One Memory

© 2016 Violetta Peters

One trip.
One journey.
One difference I could make.
My thoughts.
My fears.
My whispers when no one hears.
One touch.
One face.
One memory to take my place.

Hallelujah

© 2016 Violetta Peters

A star shines in the east over Bethlehem.
A baby lies in a manger.
It's Christmas time.
In the living room, my grandfather clock chimes,
    but I can hear those echoes in my mind.
Lord, I thank you for walking down a road
    that led from Heaven, to earth, to glory.
The evening and morning dawn.
Days move on.
Wake up, wake up, and listen to the candle
    that burned long ago.
Merry Christmas, Merry Christmas, 'tis the
    season to celebrate the birth of our King.
Hallelujah! Hallelujah!
He has come.
Bless be the name of Jesus.

Christmas Lights

© 2016 Violetta Peters

Red decorations cover our tree.
Christmas colors, blue and green.
Heavenly sounds feel the air, if you listen, if you care.
Santa's sleigh
Jingle bells
Dancer, Prancer, Donner, and Blitzen
The world should know brighten the skies with Christmas
    colors and Christmas lights.
Three wise men followed a Heavenly star.
To worship a babe.
In swaddling clothes.
Gifts of frankincense, gifts of myrrh.
A Christmas star
Heaven's heir
Red decorations cover our tree.
Christmas colors, blue and green.
Heavenly sounds feel the air, if you listen, if you care.

Christ King

© 2016 Violetta Peters

It was foretold a king would be born, and so it was
A star shined in the east over a stable in Bethlehem
Lying in a manger because there was no room in the Inn.
A baby, Christ the Holy Child of God, his name Jesus.
Born of a virgin, Mary.
His mission in life was sent on high. A mission only His love could
　　sanctify.
He is alpha and omega, the beginning and the end.
Truth and light to a dying world.
In earthly eyes He was a carpenter's son, but through
His blood flowed Heaven's reign.
Miracles of greatness.
Power devine.
In humble surroundings, but He was a king.
In the holy land of Israel, Jesus wept and carried a cross to bear our
　　sins.
The purest sacrifice for the plan of salvation and eternal life.
The sky darkened, and the earth quaked as a fearful silence
　　mourned the death of a holy king.
　　Jesus the son of the great, I AM.
He lives and forever He will reign.

Kris Kringle

© 2016 Violetta Peters

Old Kris Kringle, got holes in his pockets, got holes in his boots.
Santa needs a new pair of shoes; his old ones were good, but now
they are worn.
Snow's melting in the north, and Momma, she's tired.
Has the world gone crazy with its evil desires while the magic of
Christmas is wearing away?
Christmas began a long time ago. From generation to generation
He has kept us warm.
Jesus, the Son of God. Born in a stable beneath a shining star.
A package so bright the whole world saw the light that night.
Behold we must seek Him.
The magic of Christmas lives in our hearts.

Christmas Hope

© 2016 Violetta Peters

Christmas wishes, Christmas dreams, a joyful noise from Bethlehem.
Around the manger, a holy light.
The cry from a babe made Christmas bright.
Hope for the world.
A King is born.
A gift of love.
Heaven's joy.
Christmas stockings, Christmas toys, Santa Claus, and reindeer
   sleighs, but the greatest gift
   was the gift of life.
A gift of hope beauties bright.
Around the manger, angels sing, joy to the world, for this night our
   Savior is born,
    Christ the King.

About the Author

Violetta Peters grew up in Cecilia, Kentucky, in a small community called Howevalley, one of eight children. Her dad owned and operated a small business doing land field and bulldozer work, and was also a farmer. She has worked in a factory for 28 years and the last 20 years she has dreamed of being a writer.

She has one son, Jeremy Chad Meredith, and one grandson, Jeremy Gage Meredith, and says "my love for my son was the beginning of this journey through my childhood."

She lives in Elizabethtown, Kentucky.

Index of Poems